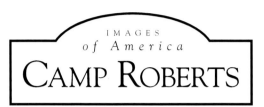

IMAGES
of America

CAMP ROBERTS

Camp Roberts is named after Medal of Honor recipient Cpl. Harold W. Roberts. After graduating from Wilmerding School in San Francisco, Roberts attended the University of California at Berkeley briefly before enlisting in the Army at Fort McDowell, California, on December 12, 1914. Following completion of basic training, he served in the Philippines and then was ordered back to California for training as a tank driver at Camp Fremont. He was subsequently shipped to France to join Company A, 344th Light Tank Battalion, of the 1st Division of the 30th Tank Brigade under Lt. Col. George S. Patton Jr. On October 4, 1918, Roberts fought in the fierce battle of Montrebreau Woods, part of the famous St. Mihiel and Meuse-Argonne Wood offensives. While advancing his tank under heavy enemy artillery fire to protect a disabled tank, his tank slid into a water-filled shell hole and became immediately submerged. Realizing that only one of the two men inside had time to escape, Corporal Roberts pushed his gunner, Sergeant Morgan, through the back door of the tank and shouted, "Well, only one of us can get out, and out you go." Despite Morgan's efforts to assist Roberts, water rushed through the tank in seconds and drowned the intrepid corporal. In addition to the Medal of Honor, Roberts was also posthumously awarded the French Croix de Guerre with Palm and the Italian War Cross.

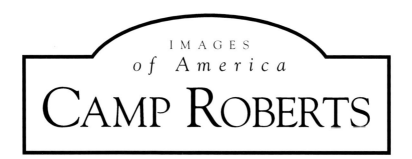

IMAGES
of America

CAMP ROBERTS

California Center for Military History

ARCADIA
PUBLISHING

George J. Albert, CPT
Charles R. Cresap, WO1
Mark J. Denger, CW2
John R. Justice, LTC
Brett A. Landis, WO1
Brett A. MacDonald, WO1
Roger D. McGrath, MAJ
Donald L. Urquidez, LTC
Daniel M. Sebby, CSM

ISBN 978-0-7385-3055-0

Published by Arcadia Publishing
Charleston, South Carolina

Printed in the United States of America

Library of Congress Catalog Card Number: 2005930170

For all general information contact Arcadia Publishing at:
Telephone 843-853-2070
Fax 843-853-0044
E-mail sales@arcadiapublishing.com
For customer service and orders:
Toll-Free 1-888-313-2665

Visit us on the Internet at www.arcadiapublishing.com

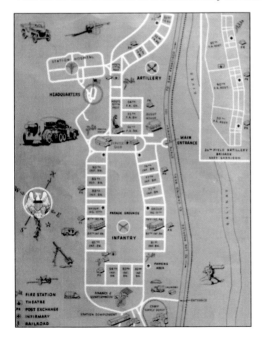

Pictured here is a layout of Camp Roberts in the early part of World War II.

CONTENTS

This book is dedicated to the one million service men and women who have trained at Camp Roberts, and especially to those soldiers who trained at the camp and later gave their last measure of devotion and courage to preserve the blessings of liberty. It is hoped that this state and nation will never forget their supreme sacrifice. This book is further dedicated to those members of the U.S. Army, Army Reserves, and California Army National Guard who currently train at Camp Roberts and to those who will do so in the future.

A military policeman is pictured here at Camp Roberts during the Korean War.

ACKNOWLEDGMENTS

Chief warrant officer Mark J. Denger, a talented military historian, once again deserves the credit for conceiving the idea of publishing our command's second in a series of photographic history books. We are indebted to him for providing the inspiration, guidance, and scholarly leadership that led to the success of this and other projects. Each chapter of this book has been written as a collaborative effort by different members of the California Center for Military History. Lt. Col. Donald L. Urquidez and WO1 Brett A. Landis, both teachers in civilian life, contributed to the initial research as well as the writing of the history of this facility. We are also beholden to Maj. Roger D. McGrath, history professor and noted author, and CW2 Denger, who contributed their time and talents to the final editing of this work.

While the photographs utilized here came principally from the collections of the California National Guard, Camp Roberts, and the California State Military Museum, we would like to extend a special thanks to John Campos of Whittier, California, for his donation of several historical World War II photographs of Camp Roberts. We also wish to thank Franco M. Federici, Derk Hale, Gary McMaster, and the staff at the Camp Roberts Historical Museum for their assistance in this endeavor. Special recognition goes to CW2 Denger and WO1 Brett A. MacDonald, who were tasked with the most time-consuming part of this work, the scanning of the hundreds of historical photographs for historical preservation as well as for their use in this book. Lt. Col. John R. Justice, who recently assumed command of the Naval History Research and Study Element, provided the necessary operational and logistics support for the southern area, and Capt. George J. Albert Jr., similarly provided operational support in the northern area of the state, each contributing their particular talents to the operational needs of this command.

On behalf of all of the members of the California Center for Military History, I wish to acknowledge the support of Arnold Schwarzenegger, governor of the State of California, and Brig. Gen. John R. Alexander, the Acting Adjutant General (TAG) of the State Military Forces, who made these opportunities possible. The California Center for Military History also extends our gratitude to Brig. Gen. (Ret.) William G. Hamilton of the California Military Museum Foundation, Brig. Gen. (Ret.) Donald E. Mattson and the staff at the California State Military Museum, Major General Walter P. Story Memorial Library and Research Center, and the Sons of the Revolution Library and Museum for their courteous assistance. Finally, I would like to express my humble gratitude to Col. Kenneth Nielsen, commanding officer, California Center for Military History and each member of this command. The dedication, devotion to duty, and talent of the members of this command has resulted in yet another fine contribution to the preservation of California's military history.

Col. Norman S. Marshall, CA SMR (Ret.)
Naval History Research and Study Element
California Center for Military History

INTRODUCTION

The story of Camp Roberts is not only a part of California's military history but also that of the Salinas Valley and Central California. It is also intimately connected with the history of Fort Hunter Liggett, immediately to the northwest.

As early as 10,000 years ago, a portion of central California became home to the ancestors of the Salinian Indians. Described as a friendly and charitable people by Spanish missionaries, the Salinians, like the better-known Chumash, spoke a Hokan language and lived in small, widely scattered groups. They hunted, gathered, and fished and, like all other Indians in California, were strangers to agriculture. Some 2,500 strong at the time of Spanish contact, the Salinians were concentrated primarily in the San Antonio and the Salinas valleys, home today to Fort Hunter Liggett and Camp Roberts. A village of Salinians was located along the Nacimiento River on today's Camp Roberts.

Although the first European contact with California came when Juan Cabrillo, a Portuguese sailing for Spain, guided his two ships into San Diego Bay in 1542, white settlement did not begin until 1769 with Gaspar de Portola's colonizing expedition. Trekking northward in search of Monterey Bay, Portola's train of men and animals passed through the area encompassed by Camp Roberts today. The journey is well described by Franciscan Juan Crespi in his famous journal and less so by Portola himself, Pedro Fages, a future governor of Spanish California, and engineer Miguel Costanso.

Spanish civilization was spread slowly and systematically from San Diego to San Francisco through three institutions: the mission, the presidio, and the pueblo. Although the first settlement was established at San Diego in 1769, Monterey was destined to be the capitol of Spanish California. The Royal Presidio of San Carlos de Monterey was founded on June 3, 1770, by Portola and Fages, six Catalonian Volunteers, four cuera soldiers, a handful of men from the ship San Antonio, and Franciscans Serra and Crespi. Following the establishment of the Monterey presidio, Portola boarded and returned to Spain.

The Presidio of Monterey was the second of four presidios that the Spanish established along the California coast. The San Diego presidio was founded the year before Monterey, the presidio at San Francisco in 1776, and the Santa Barbara presidio in 1782.

Two days after the founding of the presidio, Father Serra founded Mission San Carlos Borromeo de Carmelo, southwest of present-day Fort Ord. Named for St. Charles Borromeo, a cardinal and reformer of the 16th century, the mission became Father Serra's headquarters. Within a year Serra moved the mission five miles south to be nearer the plentiful water of the Carmel River and farther from the presidio's soldiers whose presence frightened American Indians. Now located along the river, the mission became known informally as Carmel.

During July 1771, Father Serra journeyed inland to the San Antonio valley, enthusiastically described by Portola following his journey in 1769. Hanging a church bell on an oak tree and ringing it loudly, Serra established Mission San Antonio de Padua—named for St. Anthony, a 13th century Italian scholar—on what is today Fort Hunter Liggett. The founding ceremony was attended by a Salinian Indian, earlier cajoled and given gifts by Serra. The Salinian soon returned with other American Indians eager to receive presents from the padre. Once the American Indians were attracted to the mission, it was the job of Serra and his fellow Franciscans to convert them to Christianity and instruct them in the Spanish way of life, including raising livestock and growing crops. Although occasionally suffering from drought, Mission San Antonio was among the most prosperous of the California missions and its American Indian population eventually reached 1,300. Today the mission is preserved as an 85-acre holding within the bounds of Fort Hunter Liggett.

In 1772, the indefatigable Father Serra moved south to found Mission San Luis Obispo de Tolosa in an area the Spanish called Canada de los Osos, the name inspired by the many grizzly bears roaming the locale. The Spanish hunted the bears for food, an especially important source of nourishment during the first year of settlement. The American Indians were greatly impressed by the power of the white man's guns, which could bring down a full-grown grizzly while their own arrows could not penetrate the beast's thick hide. Named for St. Louis of Toulouse, a bishop and the son of the King of Naples, the mission made the first baked brick roof tiles. The distinctive terra-cotta tiles became characteristic of the missions and of Spanish architecture in California.

With the founding of missions San Luis Obispo and San Antonio, it became necessary to build a road connecting the two missions to the Presidio of Monterey. In 1774, Col. Juan Bautista de Anza pioneered a route—a portion of which is followed by Highway 101 today—from San Luis Obispo over Questa Grade and down the Salinas Valley through Paso Robles. Anza's trail then cut through present-day Camp Roberts and Fort Hunter Liggett to Monterey. Later called "Bee Rock Road" by Americans, its path can be traced in the hills of Camp Roberts.

In 1797, Fr. Fermin Lasuen, who had replaced Father Serra as padre-presidente of the missions, founded Mission San Miguel Arcangel, named for the archangel St. Michael, the captain of God's armies or as the Spanish put it, the "most glorious prince of the celestial militia." Located only a few miles southeast of present-day Camp Roberts, Mission San Miguel originally included much of the land included in the camp today. Long before there were soldiers at Camp Roberts, there were soldiers at the missions. Each of California's twenty-one coastal missions had an escolta or military guard. The missions were connected by the "Old Mission Trail" or "El Camino Real"—the king's highway or royal road.

Despite poor soil and hot climate, Mission San Miguel, with a population of two padres, four soldiers, and 1,100 American Indians, prospered by emphasizing pastoral rather than agricultural development. In 1810, the mission had 10,558 head of cattle, 8,282 sheep, and 1,597 horses. The average annual precipitation of eleven inches was not enough to raise most crops and irrigation generally proved inadequate. Except for wheat, corn, and grapes, and small truck gardens, farming was a failure. On the other hand, livestock thrived. By 1815, the mission was supplying much of the wool used by Spanish soldiers in California.

San Miguel's vast holdings extended from the Salinas Valley to the coast at San Simeon and stretched some fifty miles north to south. In 1827, Fr. Juan Cabot reported: "From the mission to the beach the land consists almost entirely of mountain ridges . . . for this reason it is not occupied until it reaches the coast where the mission has a house of adobe . . . eight hundred cattle, some tame horses and breeding mares are kept at said rancho, which is called San Simeon. In the direction toward the south all land is occupied, for the mission there maintains all its sheep, besides horses for the guards. There it has Rancho de Santa Isabel, where there is a small vineyard. Other ranchos of the mission in that direction are San Antonio, where barley is planted; Rancho del Paso de Robles, where wheat is sown; and the Rancho de la Asunción."

Following Mexican independence from Spain in 1821, the role of the missions was dramatically reduced. In the mid-1830s, the Mexican government forced the missions to secularize and millions of acres of mission lands were transferred to mission American Indians and millions more were granted by California governors to Spanish settlers. Most of San Miguel's lands were transferred to American Indians but, as elsewhere, they quickly lost control of it. From its acreage came El Rancho Nacimiento, covering more than 42,000 acres. A hundred years later the rancho became Camp Roberts.

The town of San Miguel had its beginnings with the building of the Rios-Caledonia Adobe in 1835. The adobe served as headquarters for the area's newly appointed administrator, Ygnacio Coronel. Meanwhile, Mission San Miguel deteriorated rapidly. In 1846, Gov. Pio Pico sold what remained of the mission buildings and the once vast acreage to Petronillo Rios and William Reed for $600. Reed used the buildings for a home and a store. After the gold rush, the former mission, well positioned on El Camino Real, became an inn, then a popular saloon and dance hall. The year 1846 also saw the outbreak of the Mexican War and the Bear Flag revolt, initiated by American settlers in the Sacramento Valley. Capt. John C. Fremont, leading one of his paramilitary expeditions through the West, was camped at Marysville Buttes when the Bear Flaggers captured Sonoma and proclaimed the California Republic. Not long after, Fremont joined the revolt and took command of the Bear Flaggers. He rode south with more than a 100 armed men intending to capture California's capitol, Monterey, only to learn that the town had already surrendered to an American naval force commanded by Commo. John D. Sloat.

By the time Fremont arrived in Monterey, Sloat had been relieved by Commo. Robert F. Stockton. The new American commander promoted Fremont to major and mustered the Bear Flaggers and Fremont's men from the expedition into service as the California Battalion. Fremont led the newly formed unit from Monterey, south into the Salinas Valley. At Rancho Nacimiento, Fremont's force engaged in a running gun battle with a band of Californios. With little other opposition, Fremont quickly took control of the central coast and briefly occupied Mission San Luis Obispo before moving his troops south to Los Angeles.

The discovery of gold on the American River late in January 1848 remained a local California story for six months before word began to reach the eastern United States. By the spring of 1949, Americans were pouring into California by the thousands. San Francisco, which was known as Yerba Buena during the Mexican period and had fewer than two hundred residents, was suddenly transformed into a city. By the summer of 1949, it had a population of 5,000 residents, a year later 25,000. California's population increased as dramatically as well. As a Mexican territory, it had fewer than 14,000 residents, other than American Indians. Now, suddenly, by 1850, it had more than 100,000 residents.

The spectacular growth, transformation of society, and golden wealth was not without its problems. Crime was one of them. Along the well-traveled El Camino Real, especially in the Salinas Valley, banditos preyed upon the unwary. Some of these were prospectors who were trying their luck on the Nacimiento and Salinas rivers. The peripatetic writer J. Ross Browne reported during the summer of 1849 that El Camino Real "was infested by roving bands of Sonorans and lawless native Californians." Although California was organized as a state and admitted to the Union in 1850, lawlessness continued. The mountains of the coast range, covered with scrub oak and chaparral, and only very sparsely inhabited, offered excellent camouflage and concealment for bandits. The notorious Joaquin Murrieta had a hideout in the coast range but did most of his robbing in the mother lode country.

A particular target of the bandits were cattle buyers who came to the Salinas Valley and San Luis Obispo carrying large amounts of cash. They typically purchased cattle and drove them north to slaughter yards in San Francisco, Stockton, or Sacramento. Cattle buyers occasionally disappeared, murdered by one of the outlaw gangs that swept down upon El Camino Real. The most active gang in the region was led by Jack Powers and Pio Linares. An Irish immigrant and veteran of the Mexican War, Powers was a renowned horseman and gambler who had nerves of steel and great courage. Linares, a native of San Luis Obispo with dozens of relatives and compadres in the area, was described as "a sort of chieftain of the young Californians" of the central coast.

Just how many robberies and murders the Powers-Linares gang committed is a matter of speculation but their depredations eventually stirred the citizenry to act. During May 1858, a vigilance committee was organized at San Luis Obispo, largely by non-Hispanic Americans. Within weeks, though, nearly half of the 148 names on the committee's muster rolls were Spanish. The vigilantes' first action was to hang Joaquin Valenzuela on gallows they had erected in San Luis Obispo. Next to stretch hemp was a gang member known as El Mesteno, followed by Jose Antonio Garcia. In a blazing gun battle, the vigilantes shot to death Linares and captured two of his compadres, Miguel Blanco and Desiderio Grijalva, who were soon dangling on ropes. Still another gang member, Nieves Robles, was captured in Los Angeles and returned to San Luis to hang. Gang member Froilan Servin, unwilling to face the vigilantes surrendered to authorities in Santa Barbara. He won a change of venue to Monterey, was tried on various charges, and sentenced to San Quentin. Jack Powers escaped by steamer to Mexico.

The demise of the Powers-Linares gang, and the terror inspired among outlaws by the vigilantes, brought peace to the central coast and renewed use of El Camino Real. By the time Pres. James Buchanan returned Mission San Miguel to the Catholic Church in September 1859, a Wells Fargo stagecoach was running daily from San Luis Obispo to San Miguel and back. In 1874, Wells Fargo established an office in San Miguel. A fire razed the town in the early 1880s but a new San Miguel quickly developed north of the mission. The Southern Pacific Railroad reached San Miguel in 1886, ushering in a new era of prosperity.

Meanwhile, just south of San Miguel, the town of Paso Robles was beginning to take shape. Named El Paso de Robles (the pass of the oaks) by Spanish explorers, the site of the future town became part of a 26,000-acre land grant given in 1844 to Petronillo Rios, a retired Mexican army sergeant. In 1857, the Rios rancho was purchased for $8,000 by the brothers Daniel and James Blackburn and Drury James, the uncle of outlaw Jesse James. By the late 1860s, they had laid out the town of Paso Robles, envisioning it as a tourist resort built around the hot sulfur springs found there. They built a hotel, bathhouse, general store, and several small cottages. From these modest beginnings the town grew steadily, aided by the arrival of the Southern Pacific railroad in 1886. Farming in the region was originally devoted principally to growing wheat and barley, but grapes for wine making became an ever more important crop as the years went by.

In 1902, Congress created a commission to locate and describe sites suitable for military posts. One of the sites selected was Nacimiento Ranch, reputedly ideal for a regiment of cavalry. The U.S. Army Corps of Engineers was subsequently ordered to make a detailed survey of the ranch. The Corps reported that the area was as "healthy as any in the State of California, in addition to its mundane qualities and excellent range and training ground." Nonetheless, no action was taken until 1940 when Congress finally authorized the purchase of the ranch. Late in the fall, military contractors and construction crews went to work building "Camp Nacimiento Replacement Training Center."

At the same time, Hunter Liggett Military Reservation, since renamed Fort Hunter Liggett, was developed along the upper reaches of the Nacimiento and San Antonio rivers. Named for Lt. Gen. Hunter Liggett, a West Point graduate and veteran of the Indian Wars, the Spanish American War, and World War I, the camp was created from lands essentially donated to the War Department by William Randolph Hearst in 1940. Until 1952, the administration of the camp fell under the authority of Camp Roberts, then under that of that Fort Ord until the latter's closure in 1993. Fort Hunter Liggett today is under the authority of the United States Army Reserve Command.

One

EL RANCHO NACIMIENTO

The ranch owes its name to the river that flows through it —the Nacimiento. Fr. Juan Crespi gave the river its name in September 1769 when the Portola expedition reached its banks after crossing the formidable Santa Lucia Mountains from the coast. Reckoning that the party was close to the river's headwaters, Fr. Crespi named it Nacimiento, meaning source. A later Spanish expedition assumed the Franciscan had named the river in honor of the Nativity—another meaning for the word—and this understandable misconception gained wide currency.

An American, George Flint, first bought El Rancho Nacimiento in the early 1860s. In the mid-1870s, he built the property's original ranch house on a mesa above the east bank of the river. He also built a stable, a barn, corrals, storerooms, a granary, and a rodeo ground. Flint sold Nacimiento to an Australian rancher, A. F. Benton, who also owned a large tract of grazing lands 25 miles to the south of Nacimiento. Benton sold most of the ranch to Baron J. H. Schroeder, a German war hero, who, in 1910, sold it to Isais W. Hellman.

Under the ownership of Hellman, and the management of Fred Bixby and M. Wilson, the ranch was fully developed. By 1920, the ranch also included a cofferdam, a large reservoir, and a butcher shop to supply meat to its ranch hands and their families. After 1920, management of the ranch fell to Eli Wright, a native of the Salinas Valley. At the age of 15, Wright had worked on the ranch under George Flint, not imagining that one day he would be managing the vast spread. Wright and his family lived in the original house built by Flint until 1928, when the old house was torn down and replaced by the present ranch house.

The Army's interest in the Nacimiento Ranch began in 1901. Responding to Congressional authorization for development of military posts, a commission was created to consider Nacimiento and several other ranches in central California as sites for building camps. In 1902, in the commission's report to Congress, the Nacimiento property was declared ideal for one regiment of cavalry with excellent sites for artillery and rifle ranges. However, a Salinas Valley physician wrote to Pres. Theodore Roosevelt, stating that there were periodic outbreaks of disease in the valley and that the summertime temperatures were "90 to 120 degrees in the shade." To build a camp at Nacimiento Ranch would be a "cruel injustice to our soldiers," concluded the doctor. The letter caused the government to demand further investigation before acquisition of the land. Meanwhile, other properties moved ahead of Nacimiento for consideration.

It was not until 1940, with another world war looming, that Congress finally authorized funds to acquire the Nacimiento Ranch and build a training facility. With the exception of 450 acres that would remain in the hands of the Hellman Estate for grazing cattle, the ranch was turned over to the U.S. government during the fall of 1940. Construction of the Main or West Garrison began on November 15, 1940. Formal change of ownership, however, was not completed until early 1943.

As in the days of old, large numbers of beef cattle grazed on the vast, unfenced acreage. Hellman's managing partners, Fred Bixby and M. Wilson, pictured here on the Nacimiento Ranch in 1920s, kept a watchful eye on the herds.

When Isias W. Hellman purchased the lands that made up El Rancho Nacimiento in the 1920s, he began to build corrals, water tanks, watering troughs, and bunk houses. The original ranch house was to the left of these structures.

George Flint built the Nacimiento's first ranch house in the 1870s on the east side of the Nacimiento River. Standing in front of the old ranch house as it was being torn down in 1928 are Katherine Bixby and Mrs. Eli Wright. The Wright family had lived in the original house.

The Nacimiento's far-reaching acres included mountains and valleys, open cattle range, hillsides of California oak, and cultivated plains. It was only after Isias W. Hellman purchased the property in 1910 that, under general managers Fred Bixby and M. Wilson (1910 to 1920), and Eli Wright in the years following, the land began to take on the appearance of a working ranch.

Many activities centered on the old guest house, an important part of life on the Nacimiento Ranch.

Each year every ranch in the area would gather its cattle into corrals. Strays were then separated and calves branded to establish ownership. This usually was an occasion for festivities on the ranch. Ranch hands Eli Wright, John Rawkin, Walter Bonheim, Katherine Bixby, Wes Burnett, Tom Walker, Clint Stiltz, Fred Bixby, Don Lynch, Bill Stockdale, and a man identified only as Hotckiss prepare to gather in the herd.

After the harvest, cattle were let loose to roam on the rolling hills still covered with rich feed. The mild climate made ranches such as the Nacimiento ideal for the cattle and ranching business. Here cattle graze on the bull pasture.

The Nacimiento Ranch was fully developed and prospered under Eli Wright. He had worked on the Nacimiento under George Flint, not realizing that he would become the ranch's foreman in the 1920s.

Although the life of the vaquero gave way to the modern cowboy, many of the cowboys working on area ranches in the 1900s were direct descendants of those early California vaqueros. Pictured here are ranch hands Robert "Dinty" Moore, Fred "Slim" Basquez, Homer Turner, and Fred Kiening during harvest time.

The Nacimiento Ranch was one of California's most picturesque. Its gentle rolling hills proved to be ideal for growing grain for feed, an important part of ranching life.

Mrs. Wright is seen here with her three children at the ranch. Prior to moving to the ranch house, the Wright family had lived on a piece of land called the "White Tract," a short distance southwest of the present ranch house. They moved into the old ranch house in the 1920s when Eli Wright became foreman.

Eli Wright is seen with Steven Wilson's three sons. Both the Wright and Wilson families not only worked on the Nacimiento Ranch for many years, but Steve's sons, Elliott, Raymond "Dutch," and Lawrence "Link" Wilson also grew up on the land. Steve was a relative of one of the managing partners and had worked on the Nacimiento until 1921 when the Wilson family bought a small 250-acre ranch of their own in Kilar Canyon, just west of Paso Robles.

Two

BEGINNINGS OF A MILITARY CAMP

Construction of the main cantonment area of Camp Roberts began on November 15, 1940. Virtually all building materials had to be shipped by rail to San Miguel and then transported by truck to the construction site. Contractors used some 35 million board feet of lumber, 100 carloads of Sheetrock, and 30,600 gallons of paint. Lumber was shipped from San Miguel to a sawmill built on the camp, cut to size, and delivered directly to the sites as needed.

Plans called for 52 different types of buildings, representing 741 separate structures—barracks, mess halls, classrooms, administration buildings, fire stations, post exchanges, and churches—all of wood frame. The government required that construction be completed by March 1941.

The rapid pace of construction required at Camp Roberts called for the floors of the buildings to be laid first and then the floors used as large worktables on which the walls were framed. The walls were then raised to a vertical position, braced and nailed, and then the roof added. This system of construction, now used throughout the construction trade, was developed by the Ford Twaits Company and Morrison-Kundsen at Fort Ord. It was then perfected at Camp Roberts.

The transportation network for the camp required 188 miles of streets and roads, including nearly 75 miles of pavement. Some 250 transformers, 437 streetlights, and hundreds of poles carrying 6 different circuits on 158,200 line feet had to be installed. Telephone lines had to be strung. To meet the anticipated water needs of the camp, four wells, each 1,000 feet deep, had to be dug and three 630,000-gallon tanks built. A network of nearly 324,000 feet of water line had to be installed. Three butane plants, later converted to propane, had to be built and some 216,000 feet of gas lines laid. Rail, three and a half miles of it, had to be put down. A sewage plant had to be constructed. Building the camp was a monumental task.

Weather conditions were good when construction began in November but rain started to fall on December 16, 1940, ushering in one of the wettest winters on record. During the 199 days of construction work, there were 64 days of rain, lasting through April 1941. Some 39 inches of rain fell on Camp Roberts, more than doubling the average annual precipitation for the area. The soil was soaked to a record depth of four feet. Through rain and mud, some 8,500 civilian workmen persevered, spending 6,000,000 man-hours building Camp Roberts. The unexpected rainfall increased the cost of construction from $10,000,000 to nearly $16,000,000. This led a junior senator from Missouri, Harry S. Truman, to make a name for himself by investigating the "enormous cost overruns" associated with the construction of Camp Roberts (and nearby Camp San Luis Obispo). But the rain and cost overruns did not stop the first troops from arriving in March 1941. By the summer, the cantonment area was completed and Camp Roberts took its place as one of the largest military training facilities in the world.

From November 13, 1940, to May 16, 1941, thousands of men and machines labored to create Camp Roberts. This trencher was just one of the laborsaving devices used to build the camp.

It was a monumental task transforming the peaceful rolling hills and valleys of the huge Nacimiento Ranch into one of the largest military training centers inside the short space of 19 weeks.

Original orders in February 1941, assigning officers and cadre to Camp Roberts, termed the facility Camp Nacimiento. Battalion cadre were ordered to help complete the construction.

At that time, only about one-fifth of the facilities were ready for occupancy. The impression of the early arrivals was one of just a huge construction job. Tents and shacks for construction offices and supplies were about as numerous as buildings.

The camp's gravel pit, complete with crusher and screen, was heavily utilized following the rains.

Construction also was begun on Camp Bradley, which was renamed the East Garrison prior to its completion.

The rain began to fall on December 16, 1940, and continued until April 1941. Despite the late start and the bad weather, construction of the camp continued to progress at a remarkable rate. Taken by the 115th Observation Squadron, this photograph shows the mud and water that still remained weeks after the rains had subsided.

Rainfall recorded at Nacimiento during this period was a record 39.9 inches. With continual rain, ground conditions grew steadily worse. Nonetheless, construction proceeded on schedule.

In many places, four to six feet of mud had to be removed and replaced with dry soil. When construction began, the future site of the Infantry Parade Ground was the best location to store materials. However, this area soon turned into a sea of mud and large grading equipment bogged down. While working on the parade ground, a large "Cat" was mired up to the top of its tracks. It would take fourteen pieces of heavy equipment to get it out.

Typical of most Army camps constructed during World War II, the smallest self-contained unit in the layout of Camp Roberts was the battalion area. There were three battalions in each regimental area, which surrounded the Infantry Parade Ground. Camp Robert's Infantry Parade Ground, the length of 14 football fields, was thought to be the largest parade ground in the country.

REYURNING FROM INSPECTION
CAMP ROBERTS, CALIFORNIA

At each of the four corners of the area were the larger single-story mess halls. Between the rows of barracks, and parallel to the roads, were various service buildings. A theater and recreation building was in the approximate center of the quadrangle. Four battalion storehouses were located near the corners of the quadrangle.

This company mess hall was typical of 250-man-capacity mess halls constructed. In addition to the 84 company mess halls, seven smaller mess halls, with a seating capacity of 170 each, seven officers' mess halls in the regimental areas, and two in the hospital area were also constructed.

Row upon row of one- and two-story buildings, repeating an identical geometric design in their placement, made up the regimental area. Two paved roads ran the full length of the battalion area. In design, each battalion area was built on a quadrangle. There were two rows of 10 buildings constructed, eight of which were the two-story barracks, each facing a central compound.

At the head of the quadrangle area was the battalion administration building. Administration buildings served as the headquarters for the battalion commanders, normally commanded by a lieutenant colonel, his executive officer, a major, and the administration staff.

Barracks were constructed as semi-temporary structures on raised concrete foundations. The barrack was a two-story wood structure reinforced with heavy plasterboard and pine siding exteriors, 29 feet, 6 inches by 80 feet, which accommodated approximately 63 men.

The inside of a typical barrack is pictured here. Each barrack had a latrine complete with showers and mirrors, and was equipped with modern heating and cooling units.

Located on a high bluff to the west is "Headquarters Hill". Here, overlooking the entire camp, was general headquarters. The building housed the offices of the camp commander, the commander of the Infantry Replacement Training Center, the commander of the Field Artillery Replacement Center, and their various staffs.

When the first 320 troops began to arrive from the Presidio of San Francisco in March 1941, though, they found the camp's headquarters in one of the barrack buildings in the 91st Battalion area. It was not until April 27, 1941, that it was moved to "Headquarters Hill." Today the administration of Camp Roberts is still handled here in much the same manner as was conducted in World War II.

Located on a hillside overlooking the Infantry Parade Ground was the "Camp Roberts" sign, constructed of large rocks and painted white by soldiers in November 1941. The sign was removed the following month when the United States entered the war for fear it would identify the camp to invading aircraft. During the Korean War, the sign was restored. It was removed in later years, after practical jokers, on several occasions, rearranged the letters forming words unfit to be seen by the public from the highway.

Located just inside the main gate is the Camp Roberts sign. This sign not only serves to welcome visitors to Camp Roberts but also separated the Infantry Recruit Training Center on the left from the Field Artillery Training Center to the right.

Constructed from concrete, and rock from the Nacimiento River, a memorial plaque was placed on the wall in memory of Corporal Harold W. Roberts who the post is named after.

Located near Headquarters Hill was the "Soldiers Bowl," constructed after the California Mission style.

The Soldiers Bowl was constructed as a natural outdoor amphitheater utilizing the hillside as its bleachers. Here some 30,000 people easily can see and hear everything that happens on the stage. Not only were many troop formations held here but also performances by world-famous radio, screen, and stage stars.

The Service Club was centrally located between the Field Artillery and Infantry areas and fronted the Infantry Parade Ground. The Service Club had a fully equipped library, a piano to sing around, a soda fountain, a cafeteria, and a lounge. A second Service Club was located on the East Garrison. Also in this area was one of the camp's theaters, the bowling alley, swimming pool, tennis courts, athletic field, and the camp's sports arena.

Each regimental area had its own recreational hall or company day room, which was fully equipped with books, current magazines and newspapers, billiard and ping-pong tables, and soft drink dispensers.

Four theaters, each seating 1,038 men, brought the latest motion pictures to Camp Roberts. The admission price was only 25¢.

The camp's sports arena was located at the northwest corner of the parade ground and was fully equipped for basketball, boxing, weightlifting, badminton, and wrestling.

The camp hospital was located on a high plateau just northwest of "Headquarters Hill" to the north of the Field Artillery Recruit Training Center. The hospital facility had a commanding view of the mouth of the Nacimiento River where it empties into the Salinas. Under the watchful eye of the medical director, Col. Ralph E. Curti, the extensive hospital facility occupied a rectangular space 1,200 feet by 2,200 feet.

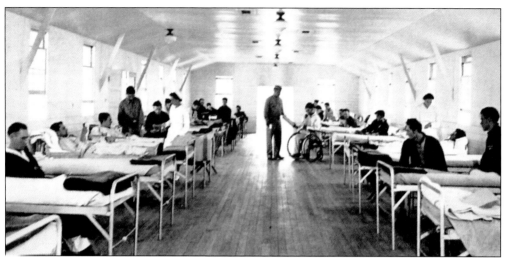

The hospital facility included a surgical theater, x-ray lab, and pharmacy. In addition to its wards and medical facilities, the hospital area had a recreation room, mess hall, power plant, and its own theater, which fell under the responsibility of the Medical Detachment, commanded by Maj. Harrison R. Bryan. Col. Leroy P. Harley, chief of the dental branch, was responsible for the dental facility. There were also housing facilities for the doctors, nurses, and support personnel.

Although the hospital is no longer operational, the services once provided there by medical personnel were indispensable. Today civilian hospitals in the area serve most medical needs.

Hundreds of these angels of mercy of the Army Nurse Corps treated all manners of medical problems, from sore throats to severe injuries.

The headquarters building for the American Red Cross was located just below Headquarters Hill. The Red Cross and Army Emergency Relief worked together to assist soldiers and their families suddenly stricken with hardship or facing emergencies. Today the building is now home to the Camp Roberts Museum.

Red Cross workers offered aid and comfort to soldiers at Camp Roberts. The Red Cross also assisted soldiers through personal and family emergencies.

The spiritual needs of the soldier were amply taken care of by the men of the Chaplains Corps who were already on the job when Camp Roberts opened in 1941. There were a total of nine chapels on post. General religious services were conducted for Catholics (chapel No. 2), Protestants (chapel No. 4), Baptists (chapel No. 5), Episcopalians (chapel No. 6), and those of the Jewish faith (chapel No. 7).

Troops in bivouac areas were afforded an opportunity to attend services in the field. Chaplains on special duty with training units were kept busy conducting worship services in the field, calling on the sick, or listening to the many tales of woe.

The interiors of the chapels were devoid of ornamentation making them serviceable for a variety of faiths. Chapel activities included baptisms, funerals, and weddings. One chapel conducted a record 121 weddings during 1943.

Several outdoor services were conducted in the Soldiers Bowl. Attended by 20,000 soldiers, the 1942 Thanksgiving service was featured in *Life* magazine.

The chapel was an especial point of interest because of the many weddings held there. A typical wedding found not only soldiers in attendance but also the parents and civilian friends of both the bride and groom.

Many weddings were small, intimate events.

Some weddings were grand affairs, hosting large numbers of civilian guests and military personnel.

Even small weddings were followed by the traditional reception.

Women's Army Corps (WAC) Headquarters building at Camp Roberts. Members of the WAC were the first women other than nurses to serve in the ranks of the United States Army.

As an auxiliary of the Army, the WAAC (Women's Auxiliary Army Corps) had no military status. Pres. Franklin D. Roosevelt signed a bill on July 1, 1943, to rectify this, and 90 days later, the WAAC was disbanded and replaced by the Women's Army Corps (WAC).

Hundreds of women served during World War II at Camp Roberts in the Women's Army Auxiliary Corps (WAAC), which later became the Women's Army Corps (WAC).

The Women's Armed Services Integration Act of 1948 permitted women into the regular Army and Reserve Corps. WAC would continue to serve in both the Korean and Vietnam Wars. The Women's Army Corps as a separate corps of the Army was disestablished on October 29, 1978, by an Act of Congress.

The quartermaster fed, clothed, and housed the soldiers at Camp Roberts. Sometimes clothing issues could be a problem.

One size did not fit all.

When Camp Roberts opened for training in March 1941, the first trainees were issued dark blue denim work fatigues and a denim field hat, similar to a sailor's cap, along with M1938 dismounted canvas leggings and a denim barracks bag—standard Army issue left over from the 1930s. Other gear included the M1 service gas mask and hood, M1910 haversack, M1910 aluminum canteen with cup and cover, and M1936 web belt.

Much of the equipment used in the first year at Camp Roberts was actually surplus from World War I or surplus as modified through the 1930s. When World War II broke out, it was a while before the olive drab field uniform and the M1 "steel pot" helmet—items generally associated with World War II soldiers—were issued to all soldiers.

The quartermaster was also responsible for the motor pool, which included garages and maintenance facilities for more than 1,000 vehicles of various kinds. In addition to 348 track vehicles such as tanks and tank destroyers, the inventory included 755 wheeled vehicles"—jeeps, sedans, cargo trucks, weapons carriers, 4-ton wreckers, 5-ton semi-trailers with tractors, and a 45-ton tank recovery truck.

One of the most utilized and versatile vehicles of both World War II and Korea was the Jeep.

The quartermaster also oversaw the camp's laundry facility. This building was a rambling structure, 180 by 270 feet. Laundry service to enlisted personnel was first offered on a cash basis: 50¢ for 12 pieces or $1 for 25 pieces. This was later changed to a flat fee of $1.50 per month, deducted directly from the soldier's pay. Each soldier was allowed to send all the laundry he wished for this one price.

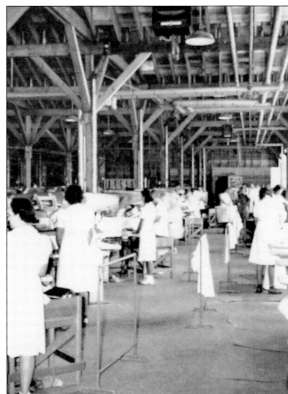

The task of overseeing the civilian men and women who worked in the camp's laundry facility fell to Capt. Walter F. Olsen. Under the auspices of the Post Exchange, nine civilian dry cleaning, pressing, and tailoring shops also operated on the post. Costs to the soldiers were moderate.

Feeding the troops was a monumental task. Brig. Gen. E. W. Fales and Maj. E. S. Curtis inspect perishable ration issue.

The quartermaster also had the responsibility to build and maintain the warehouses and cold storage plant needed for meat and vegetables as well as the camp's bakery, which had to produce 6,000 loaves of bread each day.

Maj. E. S. Curtis, QMC; Hugo Enders, administrative assistant; and staff operated the Sales Commissary, which maintained a complete stock of foodstuff; the Post Exchanges offered a large selection of merchandise. Commissary and Post Exchange cards were also available for dependents of military personnel.

Like any small city, the camp was serviced by its own gasoline station. Operated by the Post Exchange, only remnants of the station remain today.

To assist the soldiers, the Paso Robles branch of the Bank of America maintained a Camp Roberts location, south of the main gate.

With the exception of loans, normal banking services were available to the soldier.

To free soldiers for training, nearly all the work, under the direction of the camp quartermaster, was performed by civilians. Lt. Col. Harry C. Hough oversaw the massive recruiting effort undertaken by Mr. Simerman, head of civilian personnel, to fill civilian positions at the camp.

In addition to military personnel, hundreds of civilian typists, clerks, stenographers, bookkeepers, warehousemen, laundry workers, electricians, and plumbers had to be recruited and hired by the Army to maintain the camp. This recruiting truck was used by the Civilian Personnel Department from 1941 to 1945 for this purpose.

Pictured are members of the Civilian Personnel Branch. In the center in uniform is Lt. Col. Henry Hough, Commanding. To his right is Mr. Simerman, civilian in charge, whose secretary Mrs. Sutton (far right) was the mother of Betty Sutton Deverman, the first local girl to enter the Nurses Corps and one of the first nurses stationed at Camp Roberts in 1941.

The quartermaster was also responsible for the Weapons Pool and Ordnance Warehouse, which had the accounting responsibility for 24,558 M1 rifles, 1,175 Browning automatic rifles, 921 carbines, 868 pistols, 195 heavy machine guns, 172 50-caliber machine guns, 622 60-mm mortars, 144 81-mm mortars, 292 anti-tank rocket launchers, 1,539 binoculars, 25,000 bayonets, 24 57-mm anti-tank guns, and 48 105-mm howitzers. The accounting, which was handled primarily by civilian office personnel, clerks, typists, and warehouse men, was overseen by 1st Lt. H. A. Mills, 2nd Lt. G. G. Leiby, and Tech Sergeant Hofer.

The post engineer, Maj. H. A. Lyons, and a staff of over 50 personnel oversaw the maintenance and upkeep of Camp Roberts.

Several carpenters, plumbers, and tradesmen were essential camp personnel for the maintenance and upkeep of buildings and facilities.

One central fire station and three brigade fire stations provided critical fire protection at Camp Roberts. Equipment at each included both 750 gallon-per-minute and 550 gallon-per-minute pumper trucks. Pictured in front of Fire Station No. 1, from left to right, are firefighters J. Gatlon, unidentified, Vince Dailey, Gus Apruhil, and R. Bobloy.

Seen here are the men from Fire Station No. 1. Headquarters was manned by an experienced fire chief and his assistant, furnished by the U.S. Civil Service. The chief and his assistant oversaw each of the camp's four fire stations. Each station had an assignment of 15 to 18 men.

Supplies continually ran short. These civilian workers are assisting camp personnel with the camp's salvage and reclamation efforts.

Food rationing was even a problem for the military. To assist the Quartermaster Corps, soldiers from the SCU 1928 Range Detachment managed the camp's Victory Garden in an effort to have fresh vegetables for the troops.

The camp's public relations staff was especially busy as metropolitan radio stations carried the camp's entertainment programs to millions of civilian listeners each week. These radio shows were also morale builders for the huge camp audiences. Many world-renowned radio personalities came to Camp Roberts to broadcast episodes of their radio shows including Bob Hope, Jack Benny, Kay Kaiser, Edger Bergen, Charlie McCarthy, and many others. Another function of the public relations staff was producing the camp's newspaper.

Three

A PLACE TO
TRAIN SOLDIERS

Camp Roberts officially began its mission of turning raw recruits into soldiers during March 1941. Originally designated Camp Nacimiento Replacement Training Center, it was renamed to memorialize World War I Medal of Honor recipient Harold W. Roberts even before construction was completed. By the summer of 1941, the camp was fully operational and one of the world's largest military training facilities.

The Main Garrison was built to accommodate 23,000 officers and troops at any given time. The East Garrison, across the Salinas River and first occupied by the 26th Field Artillery, could accommodate an additional 6,000 troops. The camp's population peaked in 1945 when 45,000 troops were quartered in large tent cities located on the fringes of the Main Garrison. By the end of World War II, approximately 436,000 infantry and artillery troops had gone through training at either the Infantry Replacement Training Center or the Artillery Replacement Training Center on Camp Roberts. In addition to being the home of two training centers, the camp also served as an internment compound for Italian and German prisoners-of-war (POWs) during World War II. After the surrender of Italy in 1943, many of the Italian POWs remained at the camp and joined the U.S. Army's Service Units as service troops.

After decommissioning as a regular Army training site in 1946, Camp Roberts was used only by Army reserve units and by the California Army National Guard. When the Korean conflict erupted in Asia, Camp Roberts, in July 1950, was again commissioned and again became a training center for infantry and artillery units. Now under the command of the 7th Armored Division, the camp also saw the Armored Replacement Training Center established. Camp Roberts could now serve and train three types of combat arms for U.S. Army, National Guard, and Army Reserve units. During this period, classroom teaching became highly developed. Technical instruction came from teams of specialists whose mastery of particular subject areas assured professional teaching.

By the time the conflict in Korea ended in 1953, approximately 300,000 troops had passed through Camp Roberts. Once the returnee out-processing was completed in early 1954, the camp was again decommissioned as a training site and the commanding general at Fort Ord was given jurisdictional command. With the exception of the California Army National Guard, there was little troop training conducted at Camp Roberts during the Vietnam War. The camp was not officially commissioned during this period and thus earned the nickname "most active inactive post in the United States." Also during this era, a Satellite Communications Station (SATCOMSTA), the first of its kind, was constructed at Camp Roberts as part of the Army's worldwide strategic communications network. Camp Roberts was again officially closed in April 1970.

Basic training has always served as the foundation of a soldier's army service and includes such beloved pastimes as marching in squad, platoon, and company formations, in battalion and regimental parades, and training in military courtesy and discipline. Classroom instruction includes personal hygiene, military justice, first aid, individual protective measures, rules of land warfare, and employment of the armed forces. The task of training a soldier to become a skilled member of the army team is not a simple job.

These courses gave the students the fundamental training, which provided the foundation for more advanced training. Weapons training took the lion's share of time and familiarized the student with a succession of weapons: the M-1 rifle, bayonet, carbine, automatic rifle, machine gun, sub-machine gun, rocket launcher, mortar, and grenade.

Instruction included technique of operation and marksmanship on such weapons as the semi-automatic pistol, revolver, hand grenade, 60-mm mortar, 81-mm mortar, .30-caliber rifle (both Garand and Springfield), automatic rifle, light and heavy machine guns, bayonet, anti-tank and anti-aircraft guns.

Two soldiers participate in combat range training during the Korean War.

Light gun machine training is practiced during the Korean War.

Eight separate training facilities and ranges were used solely for machine gun training. Crew drill and manipulation exercises were conducted on machine gun squares of various sizes in "Sherwood Forest."

Instructors conducted both classroom and field instruction in a manner similar to a college professor. Part of each hour was devoted to lecture and demonstration and the rest to questions from students. The instructors taught 56 subjects in some 400 classes totaling nearly 700 hours during the 16 weeks of basic training. The curriculum was divided into four sections: General Subjects, Weapons, Tactics, and Battle Indoctrination.

Emphasis was also placed on teaching accuracy with the "Tank Killer," a M9A1 2.36-inch rocket launcher, and later the M20 3.5-inch rocket launcher. Each trainee fired two practice rockets at two stationary tank targets and one moving target. Sub-caliber firing of the 75-mm Recoilless rifle was conducted in the Recoilless Training Area, which was equipped with a shielded automatic moving target car capable of continually moving 12 targets back and forth at a uniform rate of speed. The area consisted of five separate facilities for practical work and concurrent training.

The spirit of the bayonet is the will to meet and destroy the enemy in hand-to-hand combat. It springs from the fighter's confidence, courage, and grim determination and results from vigorous training.

Trainees not only learned the rudiments of Army life, military drill, and interior guard duty, but also the use and care of infantry weapons. Great stress was placed on physical fitness, first aid, defense against chemical attack, map reading, and marksmanship.

The primary mission of Camp Roberts was the transformation of the trainee into an aggressive fighting soldier with confidence in his weapon and equipment and the ability to use them effectively against the enemy.

The basic assault course required five hours of instruction. Here the trainee became an aggressive bayonet fighter working his way through a tough 400-yard course, consisting of 21 obstacles and surprise targets. Another five hours of advanced bayonet training was conducted on one of two bayonet courses. Both courses were similar with ten lanes of four obstacles each. Here the trainee practiced what he learned on the basic assault course.

Chemical, Biological, and Radiological (CBR) training focused on the protective measures taken to combat CBR warfare and lasted for 10 hours. CBR training was divided among classroom, gas chamber, and the gas confidence course. The gas confidence course consisted of six obstacles, traversed by the trainee with a gas mask under simulated combat conditions.

Battle indoctrination served to prepare the soldier to withstand the psychological and physical shock of initial combat. Here the student put all of his earlier training into practice through a series of realistic training exercises, employing all the basic of techniques he had learned.

Individual training in creeping and crawling under wire, over logs, and through trenches was conducted in an area composed of four individual facilities. The Infiltration Course acquainted the trainee with the sounds and sensations of close, overhead machine gun fire and simulated enemy artillery fire. Real bullets and TNT were used to simulate actual combat conditions.

Tactics training was designed to teach students the correct way of creeping and crawling to advanced platoon and company positions.

The trainee received eight hours of hand and rifle grenade instruction. During this training period, a company was divided up into two parts—one received instruction in the hand grenade and the other in the rifle grenade. Rotation was made after four hours. The area consisted of 11 such training facilities.

Instruction was given in the technique of firing and actual field firing of the machine gun.

Mortar training was conducted at 11 facilities and ranges.

Mortar crew drill and manipulation exercises were conducted on mortar squares located in Sherwood Forest, which contained elaborate miniature mortar ranges. Training projectile ranges included simulated towns.

Map-reading instruction was conducted in five different areas.

In these areas, a trainee received instruction in the use of a map and compass on famous "Map Hill." From the hill the trainee could look down upon "real" ground forms from a 120-foot vantage point, making "Map Hill" an outstanding facility for map instruction.

In the final exam, trainees were divided into small groups and required to traverse a course using maps, aerial photographs, and a compass.

The next three training areas were designed to teach the trainee how to traverse a course by compass during both day and night in preparation for the "final" examination.

The trainee also received instruction in camouflage and concealment.

Pictured here is the combat-in-town course, providing training in "house to house" fighting that was common in Korea.

At the attack course, small infantry units were trained in assaults on limited objectives, emphasizing teamwork. Live-fire training was conducted in four specially designed areas where the trainee was taught to act as any member of the rifle squad while applying effective fire on various types of targets in offensive and defensive situations.

The combat-in-town course taught the techniques of urban warfare and the necessity and value of teamwork.

Bivouac consisted of two weeks of vigorous tactical training for the soldier. Conducted at Bear Trap Flats at Hunter Liggett, the first week of training was designed to apply all previous tactical instruction in a practical exercise under simulated combat conditions. In addition to scheduled training, the unit was under constant threat of attack by an aggressor action. During the training, the unit moves forward, advancing approximately six miles, and spends three nights occupying a defensive position, which the soldiers had to prepare quickly. Soldiers ate only field rations during the five-day week.

Conducted in "Last Chance Gulch," the proficiency test was designed to test the trainee in the most important subjects covered during the training cycle. Emphasis was placed on the recruit's M-1 rifle, automatic rifle, and machine gun. Improvements in the training program were based upon the results of this test.

Close combat courses were designed to teach aggressiveness and teamwork in destroying the enemy using weapons organic to the infantry squad.

At the conclusion of the week at Hunter Liggett, a tactical move to Camp Roberts was made by foot, and the second and final week of the bivouac commenced. Advanced and special problems were now tested. In this phase, the trainee fired live ammunition and conducted special exercises, including negotiating the small arms course and attacking a fortified position.

Located on the East Garrison, the Field Artillery Brigade was on the high mesa just northeast of and across the Salinas River from the West Garrison of Camp Roberts. It occupies a portion of the 8,000 acres purchased from the Porter estate early in January 1941. Here 250 additional buildings housed and supported approximately 6,000 trained troops assigned to the Field Artillery Brigade.

In addition to training on the .30-caliber rifle (both Garand and Springfield), automatic rifle, light and heavy machine guns, bayonet, and anti-tank warfare, the trainee learned how to fire and care for the 75-mm gun and the 155-mm howitzer.

The battle indoctrination courses were the toughest and most interesting phase of a soldier's training. Here, and in tactical problems as well, an artillery section of 105-mm howitzers, a tank platoon of 14 medium tanks, and an infantry platoon show trainees how it's done.

The leaders course was designed to select potential leaders early in their Army career. The Camp Roberts Leaders Course was capable of instructing eight classes of 90 students simultaneously. "Lead—Do not drive" was the motto of the course. Here members of the California National Guard's 49th Infantry Division take a break from training during the early 1960s.

ANNUAL ACTIVE DUTY FOR TRAINING — CAMP ROBERTS, CALIFORNIA 1958   PHOTO BY LE

In the summer of 1958, the command general of the 49th Infantry Division inspects the campaign streamers of one of the battalions.

Four

HOLLYWOOD COMES TO CAMP ROBERTS

During World War II, movie stars and entertainers arrived at Camp Roberts to bring cheer to the troops and boost their morale. Maintaining good morale was no small task. The daily grind of hard training, life in tents and barracks, separation from loved ones, and anticipation of battle overseas weighed heavily upon the soldiers. Their devotion to duty and sacrifices were recognized and appreciated by a number of stars who made certain to visit the soldiers and bring them a brief respite from the challenges they faced daily. Hollywood also made training films and war movies as part of the war effort. Moreover, several established stars, such as Clark Gable, Jimmy Stewart, and Tyrone Power, enlisted in the armed forces and faced the enemy in battle. Those who couldn't fight, sang and danced their way into the hearts of American troops, both here and abroad.

The United Service Organization (USO) was formed in response to a 1941 request from Pres. Franklin Roosevelt, who thought it best if private organizations handled the on-leave entertainment for the rapidly expanding armed services. Hollywood stars were not the only ones to respond. Local civilian volunteers joined with silver screen sirens in serving and entertaining the soldiers at Camp Roberts and at local USO clubs—an activity that became the focus of many films.

The USO made history with its campaign of entertaining the troops with traveling "camp shows." The role of the Hollywood celebrity in these shows was indispensable. Camp Roberts had the honor of hosting the first show, staged before 20,000 troops at the newly constructed outdoor theater called the "Soldiers Bowl." The show featured the great film comedy team of Stan Laurel and Oliver Hardy, and comedian Red Skelton, who would return to Camp Roberts in 1944 as a soldier himself. From that first show on, a parade of stars came to entertain the troops at Camp Roberts. The list of stars that performed at Camp Roberts reads like a Hollywood's who's who. Opera, theater, and radio performers also lent a hand. NBC and CBS aired several of their network radio shows from the camp. Even some episodes of Sherlock Holmes, enthralling listeners throughout the nation, originated at Camp Roberts. Many other radio shows were broadcast only to the soldiers on the post as rehearsals. Other forms of entertainment and recreation, including dances offered at the post's Service Club, sporting events at the camp's many recreation halls, and movies at one of the camp's theaters helped to fill what little free time the soldier had.

The efforts of the USO, Hollywood, and the many civilian volunteers will never be forgotten. They will live on in the memories of the thousands of soldiers who once lived and trained in the now abandoned barracks of Camp Roberts. These soldiers, and Hollywood, both served their country in her time of need and now Camp Robert stands as a tribute to them all.

Donald O'Connor was one of many entertainers to appear at the Camp Roberts Soldiers Bowl during the war. O'Connor was assigned to Special Services and entertained the troops until his discharge in 1946. He returned to films in 1947. Before the war, O'Connor was best known for his role as Bing Crosby's younger brother in the amiable family musical, *Sing You Sinners* (1938) and as Huckleberry Finn in *Tom Sawyer, Detective* (1939). He appeared in no fewer than 19 films in 1940. After the war and at the height of his powers as a light comedian, he was cast as Cosmo Brown in *Singin' in the Rain* (1952), directed by Stanley Donen and costarring Gene Kelly. The film included a scintillating song and dance performance of "Make 'em Laugh." O'Connor later starred in six films with Francis, the Talking Mule. Peggy Ryan is seen here with O'Connor.

One of the first actresses to appear on stage at the Camp Roberts Soldiers Bowl was the talented actress and singer Vivian Blaine (Vivian Stapleton). She was also an accomplished nightclub performer and band singer by the time 20th Century Fox had signed her in 1942, and the only person to share top billing with Laurel and Hardy in *Jitterbugs* (1943), considered by many to be the duo's best film.

Entertainer, composer, songwriter, producer, and actor George Jessel, appearing here with actress Doris Merrick, often served as master of ceremonies. This earned him the sobriquet "Toastmaster General of the United States."

Dinah Shore (Frances "Fanny" Rose Shore), best remembered as the hostess of daytime talk shows from the early 1950s through the late 1970s, was a popular big band singer and star of radio in the late 1930s. She was appearing in feature films by the mid-1940s, having taken her stage name from a popular song, "Dinah."

The Camp Roberts Rodeo was an annual tradition throughout the 1940s. Professional cowboys joined with amateurs and soldiers in the true rodeo fashion.

The rodeo was a favorite form of entertainment among the local boys, and a keen competition seemed to exist between them and some of the boys from the Midwest. A few soldiers had previous ranch or rodeo experience, but most had little or none. All, however, enjoyed the show.

Special guest stars such as Gene Autry (Orvon Gene Autry) made appearances to the rodeo. Stars the caliber of Autry drew even local townsfolk to see the show. The tradition set by the rodeos still continues, although now the annual rodeo is held at the mid-state fairgrounds in Paso Robles.

When World War II broke out, Gene Autry was determined to join the armed forces and do his part. On July 26, 1942, during a live broadcast of his radio show "Melody Ranch," and at the Pentagon's request, he was inducted into the Army Air Forces as a technical sergeant. He went on to become a C-47 pilot, once flying the "Hump" over the Himalayas from India to China. Autry is the only person to be honored with five stars on the Hollywood Walk of Fame.

The USO performed many services, including staffing an information booth, providing soldiers with notices of off-duty activities on and off post, and transportation schedules.

Two USOs, one in Paso Robles and the other in San Miguel, were within easy reach of the soldiers of Camp Roberts. Both clubs offered services such as lunch and soda counters, recreation rooms, outside volleyball courts, ping-pong tables, libraries, dances, and entertainment.

The USO was more than just Hollywood entertainers. The clubs were operated by local men and women who provided the soldiers with fresh coffee and refreshments.

The USO also sponsored many of the camp's dances, both on and off post. Local girls volunteered to give the soldiers a break from their normal routine. Many of these dances featured live music that varied as much as did the performers. Slow ballads, which were extremely popular, were often played alternately with a fast "jump" tune, such as the "Lindy Hop."

In addition to off-post USO dances and shows, many off-duty activities centered around the camp's recreation halls. Here soldiers could listen to weekly radio broadcasts performed at other camps.

These recreation centers provided a cool place for the soldiers to unwind and to grab a bite of food and a cold drink.

Large and small ensembles toured Camp Roberts under the aegis of the USO, exposing the troops to various genres of music. Popular music included the boogie woogie, stride, and the barrelhouse, or fast western.

Bands and orchestras were considered a vital part of the war effort. During World War II, two styles of performance predominated: "sweet" bands such as those led by Russ Morgan, Eddy Duchin, Guy Lombardo, Kay Kaiser, and Tommy Tucker, and "jump" bands with Benny Goodman, Tommy Dorsey, or Artie Shaw out front.

Kay Kaiser and his "College of Musical Knowledge" was among the most popular of the big bands to perform at Camp Roberts. The recording industry soon became aware of what Kaiser had dubbed "GI Nostalgia," that special longing for home and the girl left behind. In addition to leading his band during the war years, Kaiser starred on a light-hearted radio show.

Camp Roberts also had the distinction of being the only military base in the United States with its own opera house. Vladimir Rosing introduced the soldiers to the world of opera, having his performers sing in English and billing the operas as musicals. Rosing's productions were known for their large numbers of women performers, which soldiers did not find objectionable. "The boys saw a show of girls, beautiful music, comical situations and lots of laughs," said the Camp Roberts newspaper in a review of *The Merry Widow*.

Red Skelton (Richard Skelton) was one of the first to bring much-needed laughs to Camp Roberts. It was during this period that Skelton began developing various comedic characters. His vaudevillian act consisted of pantomimes, pratfalls, funny voices, crossed eyes, and numerous sight gags that came to identify Skelton in his entertainment career. He would later come back to Camp Roberts as a soldier.

When Private Skelton arrived at Camp Roberts, his fellow soldiers tacked a sign on his barrack that read: "Tour a Movie Star's Home. Twenty-Five Cents!" Although most movie stars became officers, Skelton was content with the title of "Camp Roberts Most Famous Private." After completing basic training, he was assigned to the Camp Roberts entertainment section, where he entertained the troops. By the end of the war, Red Skelton had more than 600 military appearances at military posts and hospitals to his credit.

Pvt. Robert "Mitch" Mitchum received an Oscar nomination for his role as Lt. Bill Walker in *The Story of GI Joe* just before he was inducted and sent to Camp Roberts for basic training with the 3rd Platoon, Company A, 76th Infantry Training Battalion. He later served at Fort MacArthur and was promoted to private first class before being discharged with the war's end. After the war, his rugged good looks, deep voice, and casual manner made him a box office hit.

Pvt. William Holden (William Franklin Beedle Jr.) is well known for his action roles in *Stalag 17* (1953), *The Bridges at Toko-Ri* (1954), *The Bridge on the River Kwai* (1957), and *The Wild Bunch* (1969); although his best movie may be *Sunset Boulevard* (1950). Enlisting in 1942, completing basic training at Camp Roberts, and later graduating from Officer Candidate School, he was assigned to the Army Air Force where he made training films until 1945. The adjutant of his unit was Capt. Ronald Reagan, and a roommate was baseball great Hank Greenberg. Holden later was the best man at Reagan's wedding. Holden's brother Bob, a naval aviator, was killed in the Pacific January 1, 1944.

LT. Wᵐ F. HOLDEN

Each week Garland sang, engaged in repartee with Hope, and participated in many of the comedic skits on Hope's radio show. Her most memorable line endeared her to the soldiers: "Are you sure you'll feel at home on this program?" asked Bob Hope. "Oh, yes, Mr. Hope . . . you should have seen the strange creatures I worked with in *The Wizard of Oz*."

Bob Hope broadcast many a radio show from Camp Roberts. He would usually set up in either the Sports Arena (today known as the main gym across the street from the Museum) or movie theater No. 1, just north of the Main PX. Here his many guests became part of Hope's famous Pepsodent Show. Judy Garland, who had starred in the *The Wizard of Oz* (1939), was a regular cast member of the show.

One of the more memorable radio broadcast from Camp Roberts featured Bob Hope and his special guest star, Jane Russell, who had recently costarred with Hope in the western-comedy, *The Paleface*. The beautiful and voluptuous Russell was one of the soldiers' favorite Korean War–era stars. Bob Hope, the master of puns, introduced her as "the two and only, Miss Russell."

The beautiful, blond German native Marlene Dietrich wowed the troops at Camp Roberts on several occasions. Dietrich made a large mark in the war effort, performing the favorite "Lilli Marlene" on USO tours and recording anti-Nazi propaganda in German. She was later awarded the Medal of Freedom and Chevalier of the French Legion of Honor after the war.

At left, the most celebrated "pin-up girl" to appear at Camp Roberts was actress Betty Grable (Elizabeth Ruth Grable). Although she never toured outside the United States for the USO, Grable actively participated in war efforts, appearing at military camps and bond rallies where she would auction off her nylons. World War II was underway when Lucille Ball (right), along with her husband Desi Arnaz, appeared at Camp Roberts encouraging soldiers to buy war bonds. Known as "Queen of the B's" in the 1930s, Lucille Ball would later become the "First Lady of Television" and one of America's greatest comediennes. *I Love Lucy* quickly made her a household name and kept generations of Americans laughing. In 1989, she was posthumously awarded the Presidential Medal of Freedom.

Ventriloquist Edger Bergen's skill and humor made him and his characters famous even though radio rendered his wooden friends invisible to their audience. Bergen shared the spotlight with dummies Charlie McCarthy and Mortimer Snerd, much to the delight of the soldiers. The star of the show was unquestionably Charlie McCarthy, the perpetual eighth-grader in a top hat and monocle who had a seemingly endless supply of racy come-ons and witty insults. But even Mortimer J. Snerd got a jab or two in once in awhile.

Hollywood icons Stan Laurel and Oliver Hardy were among the performers who starred in the first Hollywood Revue Camp Show held at the Camp Roberts Soldiers Bowl.

Many of the radio broadcasts would feature Camp Roberts soldier talent as well as celebrity guests. Nearly everyone, including unit commanders, wanted to take center stage.

Talent contests were held for the soldiers. If a comedy skit or talent was selected, a soldier might appear on a radio show broadcast from the camp. Unfortunately, audiences often had to first suffer through cornball jokes in a comedy skit.

Even when there were no women entertainers around, it didn't stop these guys, who simply improvised.

The broadcasts were a great break for the soldiers, and sent Camp Roberts over the airwaves to homes and families across the nation. Some of the shows were nothing more than spoofs from movies.

Barbershop music was indeed developed from informal gatherings of amateur singers in such unpretentious settings as the local barbershop. Often characterized as four dandies, bedecked with straw hats, striped vests, and handlebar mustaches, the barbershop style of harmony was not limited to the quartet and was a quaint symbol of small-town Americana.

Practice . . . practice . . . practice.

During the Korean War as well, musical programs ranged from formal military music to the popular music of the day.

Military bands and music ensembles have been an integral part of armies around the world for hundreds of years. The U.S. Army has employed bands to enliven marches and boost morale ever since the American Revolution. The Field Artillery Replacement Training Center (FARTC) band worked at various locations on Camp Roberts during World War II. The band, along with the Infantry Replacement Training Center (IRTC) band, would play at graduation ceremonies, religious services, formal shows, and impromptu gatherings.

Boxing matches were often held at Camp Roberts with service men participating, many of them former professional or amateur champions. Joe Louis, heavyweight champion, was drafted during World War II. His principal duty was refereeing boxing matches at Army posts.

Joe Louis's first appearance at Camp Roberts was at the Soldiers Bowl where he refereed matches featuring the camp's soldiers.

The heavyweight champ also appeared in the ring where a few soldiers had the opportunity to spar with him for a round or two.

Joe Louis's appearances helped blacks in the Armed Forces break racial barriers during the 1940s. By the end of the Korean War, the U.S. Army and National Guard were fully integrated.

Even to this day, actors such as Mel Gibson come to Camp Roberts. He and a host of other actors came to the camp to film *We Were Soldiers* (2002), a movie based on the book *We Were Soldiers Once and Young* (1992), written by Lt. Gen. Harold G. Moore (Ret.) and Joseph L. Galloway. Battle scenes were filmed at Camp Roberts and nearby Fort Hunter Liggett. In addition to renting an assault vehicle land bridge, Huey helicopters, and trucks from the California National Guard, more than 600 California Army and Air National Guardsmen took part in the filming as movie extras.

Five

"THANKS FOR THE MEMORY"

Commonly called "Camp Bob" by the soldiers who trained there, Camp Roberts was visited often by legendary comedian Bob Hope. Quipped Hope in a 1952 radio broadcast from the camp: "It's always a special personal thrill to play at Camp Roberts. I've played a lot of Army camps but this is the only one that they named after me." Hope made Camp Roberts his own and left indelible memories in the troops who watched him perform.

As the United States armed forces trained for possible entry into World War II, Bob Hope broadcast his Pepsodent Show on May 6, 1941, from March Army Air Field in Riverside. It was the first time a radio show originated from a military installation but would be followed by many more such broadcasts. During World War II, nearly every one of Bob Hope's Pepsodent Show broadcasts originated on location in front of an audience of soldiers. Dozens of shows originated at Camp Roberts. Hope said he was "so exhilarated" by the receptions given him by the troops that he "became a compulsive entertainer for the forces." By the end of 1953, Bob Hope had performed before a million servicemen and women at some 400 camps, naval stations, and military hospitals around the world. Bob Hope concluded most of his broadcasts and personal appearances with the show tune, "Thanks for the Memory," which was introduced in the film *Big Broadcast* of 1938. He made the tune his signature song and often modified the lyrics to fit a particular audience of troops. For soldiers at Camp Roberts and elsewhere, the song and Hope were inseparable.

A true American patriot at heart, Bob Hope had tried to enlist in 1941 but he was already nearly forty years old and was told he could be of more use as an entertainer. For more than 60 years he did just that, traveling the world and entertaining U.S. troops wherever they were stationed. His 1966 Vietnam Christmas show, when televised, was watched by an estimated 65 million people, the largest audience of his career. He brought to the troops the well wishes of the American people and laughs that they so sorely needed. He was still doing the job during the Gulf War, performing before American troops in Saudi Arabia. By then, he had entertained so many troops in so many war zones that he had a standard joke for the times he was interrupted by gunfire: "I wonder which one of my pictures they saw?"

His tours of duty during World War II, Korea, Vietnam, the cold war, and the Gulf War earned him the title of "honorary veteran," bestowed upon him by an Act of Congress in 1997. Upon receiving the award, Hope said: "I've been given many awards in my lifetime—but to be numbered among the men and women I admire most—is the greatest honor I have ever received." Upon hearing the news of his death on July 27, 2003, Camp Roberts's flag was lowered to half-mast in honor of the camp's greatest "war" veteran.

The passing of Bob Hope on July 27, 2003, marked the end of an era. Of all the stars who performed at Camp Roberts, he was the first and last link to the birth of the entertainment industry as we know it today. He had a soldier's profound sense of patriotism.

Bob Hope was a vaudeville star, Broadway star, movie star, radio star, comic book hero, an author, producer, recording star, and the ultimate USO cheerleader. As a vaudeville stage performer, he climbed the ladder of success to become a song and dance man and ultimately a headliner. Broadway made use of his soft-shoe routines and, when Hollywood called for him in 1934, he never left. He appeared on countless radio programs and, during the 1950s, even in his own comic book published by DC Comics. He was one of the first television pioneers. Later in his career, he would "play" himself in over 150 specials broadcasts.

Six

THE NATIONAL GUARD TAKES OVER

The California National Guard spearheaded a drive for Camp Roberts to be reactivated as a much needed training and mobilization site for its forces. On April 2, 1971, under an agreement with the U.S. Army, Col. Glenn Muggleberg assumed responsibility for the camp on behalf of the State of California. Since then, Camp Roberts has been used for training by every service component, both active and reserve, and a host of government agencies and civilian groups. While the camp itself remains federal property, all activity is under the administration of the California National Guard and the Office of the Adjutant General (OTAG).

During the last decade, as federal training facilities throughout California have been closed or greatly curtailed, the high quality of field and garrison facilities at Camp Roberts, and its central location, continues to make it one of the best training sites in the country. The camp today supports light and heavy maneuver (mounted and dismounted), live-fire training, aerial gunnery, drop zones, and helicopter operations on two airfields. It also supports the Regional Training Site-Maintenance (RTS-M), the Mobilized and Training Equipment Site (MATES), an Organizational Maintenance Shop (OMS), and provides all training support including billeting, dining, administration, and community relations. Camp Roberts further supports field and light infantry tactical training as a Maneuver Training Center (MTC) and rapid mobilization of National Guard troops as a State Operated Mobilization Site (SOMS).

Virtually all elements of the California National Guard have taken advantage of Camp Roberts. It has been extensively utilized by the 40th Infantry Division (mechanized), California Army National Guard, an armor-heavy mechanized infantry division that was first raised during World War I. Camp Roberts's storage and field exercise areas, workshops, firing ranges, driving courses, drop zones, and helicopter airfields provide outstanding training opportunities for infantry, artillery, armor, and transportation units preparing for their military missions.

In addition to the California National Guard, Camp Roberts is utilized for training by the U.S. Army, Army Reserves, Marine Corps, Navy, and Air Force. It is the scene of activities for a great variety of units and organizations, from Army Special Operations groups to multistate task forces to local law enforcement agencies.

Since September 11, 2001, and the subsequent wars in Afghanistan and Iraq, the value of Camp Roberts has been demonstrated again, especially in supporting the mobilization of National Guard units for both domestic and overseas missions. Camp Roberts continues to work hard at serving the State of California and the nation.

Since Camp Roberts was reactivated in 1971 as a field and light infantry tactical training center, it has become the primary home training ground for the 40th Infantry Division (mechanized), California National Guard. The 40th is well known and respected for its deeds and exploits during World War II and Korea.

The 1970s ushered in a period of transformation for the California National Guard. As America was entering the "all-volunteer era," the guard became integrated under the military's "Total Force Policy," resulting in more missions, equipment, and training opportunities than ever before. The Army's "affiliation" program soon teamed National Guard units with active Army combat units to train and later deploy.

The "Total Force Policy" has caused the California National Guard to become one of the most heavily tasked military forces in our nation's arsenal. As a result, Camp Roberts has been transformed to meet the needs of guard units deploying in response to new and different threats. Whether in support of peacetime or wartime training missions, homeland security, riot suppression, counter-drug trafficking, or disaster preparedness and response, Camp Roberts continues to respond to the needs of the troops.

The utilization of Camp Roberts as a training ground for California guardsmen has enabled the California National Guard to alert, federalize, and rapidly deploy personnel and equipment to any theater of operation.

Like other federal and state training facilities, Camp Roberts continues to evolve. Camp Roberts offers real-world training conditions to meet the ever-changing needs of today's National Guard.

Live-fire exercises like this on former World War II tank and howitzer ranges affords realistic training even against tanks and armored personnel carriers which are designed to get soldiers to the front with minimum exposure to injury.

To maintain their proficiency, Special Forces and Rangers utilize many of the older buildings for their training needs.

As in the days of World War II and the Korean War, Camp Roberts offers realistic infantry training facilities to meet the ever-changing role of the National Guard.

As different types of training intensify so too does modernization of facilities. This battle-ready guardsman has a thermal weapon sight-mounted on his M-16 rifle that provides a clear and steady view of his target. To accommodate such needs, Camp Roberts recently built a state-of-the-art 1,000-yard sniper range for Special Forces and Rangers.

Camp Roberts's 40,000 acres allow for training exercises for a broad range of soldier skills in a combat-simulated environment, essential for today's war fighter.

Camp Roberts's rolling hills and valleys not only provide valuable training areas for infantry but also for heavy assets such as the M1A1 Abrams tank.

To further support training and deployment capabilities, the East Garrison is now home to the Mobilization and Training Equipment Site (MATES). A relatively modern facility, MATES is where all heavy assets of the 40th Infantry Division are maintained, stored, and issued to battalions for training or deployment by rail. At MATES are some 200 M1A1 Abrams tanks, 100 155-mm self-propelled howitzers, 100 M2A2 infantry fighting vehicles, 400 more tracked combat and support vehicles, 400 heavy truck and wheeled vehicles, and 2,000 small arms, mortars, and 25-mm automatic cannon.

A Satellite Communications Station (SATCOMSTA) was constructed on Camp Roberts during the Vietnam era as part of the Army's worldwide strategic communications network. Today SATCOMSTA operates communication traffic for Pacific-fixed stations as part of the Defense Department's Communications Satellite Ground Terrain Service.

To the casual observer, Camp Roberts looks as though it is an inactive post. Many of the barracks and chapels have fallen in disrepair and are being selectively demolished. At the same time, however, other buildings are undergoing refurbishing and modernization, including the regional maintenance training site

As these 184th Infantry soldiers qualify with their weapons on ranges originally built for World War II soldiers, today's National Guard soldiers are continually training and preparing for war in a facility that is deeply rooted in its past.

With the smoke still rising from the rubble of the World Trade Center towers in Manhattan, on September 13, 2001, National Guard and Reserve troops were called up for homeland defense and civil support missions. A State Operated Mobilization Site (SOMS), Camp Roberts was transformed into a center of activity within hours. With relatively little public notice or fanfare, Soldier Readiness Processing (SRP) was soon underway in support of these historic deployments.

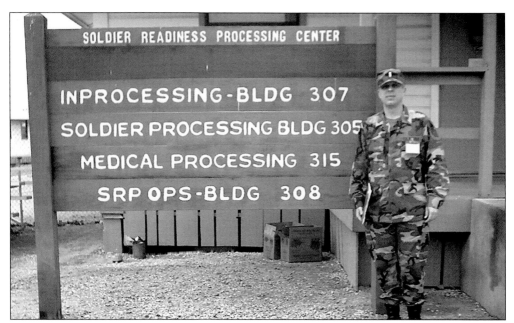

Camp Roberts is the mobilization nerve center for the California Army and Air National Guard. Not since the Korean War has Camp Roberts played such an important role in the security of this state and nation as thousands of National Guard troops are continually processed through Camp Roberts.

Expedited mobilization activities at Camp Roberts, traditionally done at active-duty Army installations, improved rapid deployment of the California National Guard into theaters of operation.

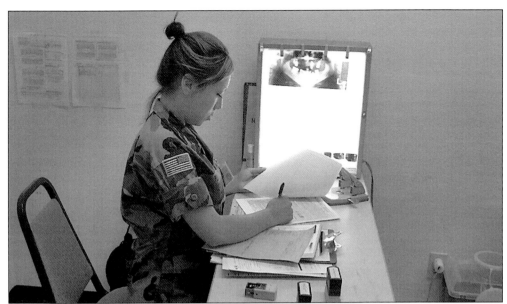

Although the California National Guard remains a "minuteman" force, since 1996 the state's citizen-soldiers have been often called to federal active duty. This trend has served to expand the mission scope of Camp Roberts as the mobilization center for the California National Guard. Soldier Readiness Processing at Camp Roberts may not be a glamorous job but since September 11, it has become one of the most critical.

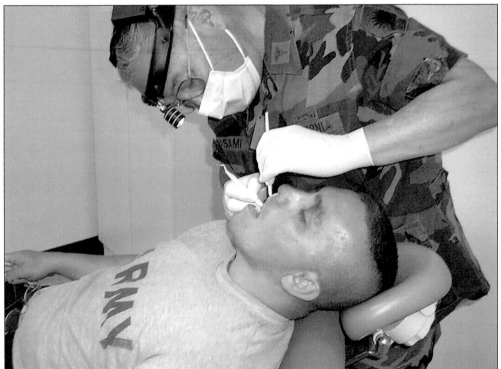

Soldier Readiness Processing is an important job entailing briefings, physical and dental exams, preparing wills, updating personnel records, and many other labor-intensive administrative duties.

At a steadily increasing operational tempo, Camp Roberts, thanks to a few dedicated soldiers, continues to support the vital role of soldier readiness, whether in support of peacekeeping or wartime missions, including the global war on terrorism.

Camp Roberts continues to make certain that our state military forces are always ready and always there, ensuring the safety and security of our states and nation.

Maj. Gen. Thomas Eres, the Adjutant General of California, views the Freedom Fountain, a restored fountain originally built by Italian prisoners-of-war who were confined at Camp Roberts during World War II. The fountain was recently rededicated to the memory of California National Guard soldiers lost in the global war on terrorism.

Seven

MUSEUM AND HISTORICAL PRESERVATION

As Camp Roberts continues to undergo revitalization and rehabilitation of its training facilities and training areas, we risk losing key elements of our state's military history. This presents both an interesting and significant challenge to the State of California and the state Military Department: How can historical artifacts at the camp be preserved while improving the camp's ability to support the current military mission?

As a historic site, Camp Roberts possesses all of the elements needed to put the state's military heritage on display. Through the development of an "in house" historical preservation plan, it is hoped that the state will preserve this rich history through recognition of several of the camp's historical structures and artifacts, and the creation of a depository for all documents related to the camp and its soldiers.

Developing a comprehensive historical preservation program for Camp Roberts remains a challenge due to the limited resources available and the funding requirements for such an effort. Funding is desperately needed to support historians, archivists, and curators dedicated to the success of this mission.

The first step in the historical preservation of the camp has already been taken with the establishment of the Camp Roberts Historical Museum and Museum Annex. This initial effort allows the history of the camp to be shared with the soldier and general public alike. Our goal is to expand the museum, making it possible to display a wide variety of historical artifacts currently in storage and unseen by the public, to categorize and index all relevant historical documents and photographs, and to increase hours of operation. Ideally the museum will become a facility used and enjoyed by veterans of Camp Roberts, historians, students, and the general public.

All interested parties can help make the preservation of the history of Camp Roberts come true by contributing to the Camp Roberts Museum Fund. The museum is operated under the umbrella of the California State Military Museum and the California Military Museum Foundation, a 501(c)(3) non-profit organization, which is dedicated to preserve and protect the legacy of our soldiers who have trained at Camp Roberts. This project is a joint effort of the California State Military Museum, California Center for Military History, and the Camp Roberts Historical Museum. For further information, please write:

> Camp Roberts Historical Museum
> Bldg. 114
> Camp Roberts, California 93451-5000

> or visit us on the web at: www.militarymuseum.org

Originally the American Red Cross headquarters at Camp Roberts, building 114 was converted to house the first National Guard Garrison Commander, Col. Glenn Muggleberg, and his family during the 1970s. In later years, the building served to house visiting general officers. It was given to the Camp Roberts Historical Museum in April 1993, and currently serves as the museum's main complex.

Once inside the main museum's entryway, visitors are greeted by sights and sounds from an era long past. Visitors can hear one of Bob Hope's radio broadcasts that was aired from the camp as they pass the museum's gift shop. The museum also contains a small reference library and a video viewing room where visitors can watch camp documentaries.

To the right of the entrance is a display honoring Cpl. Harold W. Roberts. Included among his other decorations is the Medal of Honor.

Hundreds of photographs line the walls, each telling its own story.

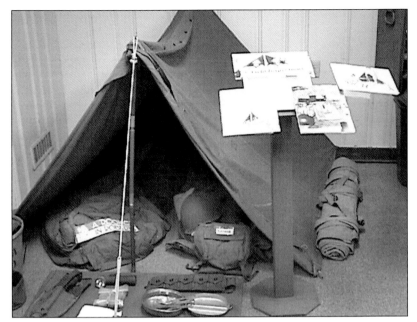

This exhibit graphically demonstrates what soldiers during World War II carried into the field and used on a typical five-day bivouac.

This vintage field table, complete with portable typewriter and field telephone, demonstrates how some technology has advanced. Displays and exhibits like these take the visitor through each period of Camp Roberts development —from the days of El Rancho Nacimiento to the camp's construction, through World War II, the Korean War, Vietnam, and the Gulf War, to the present.

Every era had distinctive uniforms.

Typical barrack life during World War II is on display in this exhibit, proving to the modern-day soldier that some things have not changed at Camp Roberts.

The old post office building, building 6485, served as the original home of the museum. Today it serves the camp as the Museum Annex. Here visitors can view the museum's large vintage vehicle collection as well as other exhibits and displays.

Inside and outside the Museum Annex can be found relics of years past. A few of the vehicles on display include the prototype of the "Bradley" mechanized infantry fighting vehicle, M7 "Priest" 105-mm self-propelled howitzer, M41 "Walter-Bulldog" light tank, and M47 "Patton" medium tank, just to name a few.

The museum's collection of armored vehicles, such as this half-track, rival collections in the Armor Museum named for Gen. George S. Patton Jr. at Fort Knox, Kentucky. Best of all, there's no admission charge at Camp Roberts.

An M4 "Sherman" on display at Camp Roberts.

The California State Military Museum is a part of the United States Army Museum System and is the official military museum and historical research center for the State of California. Its headquarters are located just blocks from the state capitol, in the Old Sacramento Historical Park, and the museum is operated for the California State Military Department by the California Military Museum Foundation, an IRS 501(c)(3) non-profit educational organization, and is supported by the California Center for Military History (CCMH). A major command of the California State Military Reserve (CA SMR), the CCMH provides support to the California National Guard's historical, command information, recruiting, and community relations programs, and provides augmentation services for the California State Military Museum as an affiliate activity of the U.S. Army Center of Military History.

The Major General Walter P. Story Library and Resource Center, located in the basement of the California State Military Museum in Sacramento, has one of the finest collections of military histories in the western United States with over 10,000 volumes. The California State Military Museum also operates four satellite museums: Camp Roberts Historical Museum and Museum Annex; Camp San Luis Obispo Military Museum and Historical Site; the 40th Infantry Division Museum at the Joint Forces Training Center (Los Alamitos); the 185th Armor and 251st Coast Artillery Regimental Museum (San Diego). In addition, the California State Military Museum maintains the Fresno Air National Guard Base Historical Site. Since the National Guard has a history beginning with colonial America and the Revolutionary War, the California State Military Museum is also affiliated with the Sons of the Revolution Library and Museum located in Glendale, California, and is supported by the Naval History Research and Study Element of the California Center for Military History.

The California State Military Museum works to improve public awareness of the importance of California's military contributions to the local community, state, and nation. It proudly serves the general public, students, historians, and members of the armed forces in the preservation of military history for present and future generations. For further information, please write:

> California State Military Museum
> 1119 Second Street
> Sacramento, California 95814
>
> or
>
> California Center for Military History
> 8400 Okinawa Street
> Sacramento, California 95823
>
> or visit us on the web at www.militarymuseum.org